CROSSROADS:
AN ANTHOLOGY OF WRITING FROM ABERYSTWYTH UNIVERSITY'S CREATIVE WRITING MA 2025

The Aberystwyth University Creative Writing MA course sees students engage in workshops, critical and creative discussions, and preparation for future careers in the literary field. This anthology was curated, edited, and launched by students completing their Master's in 2025 as an optional component of their 'Writer as Professional' module. The contributors to the anthology include current and past MA students, as well as Creative Writing Undergraduates. For many of those included, this is their first opportunity to be published.

© 2025, Broken Sleep Books. All rights reserved; no part of this book may be reproduced by any means without the publisher's permission.

ISBN: 978-1-917617-89-5

The author has asserted their right to be identified as the author of this Work in accordance with the Copyright, Designs and Patents Act 1988

Cover designed by Aaron Kent

Edited by Iestyn Tudor

Typeset by Aaron Kent

Broken Sleep Books Ltd
PO BOX 102
Llandysul
SA44 9BG

CONTENTS

FOREWORD 7

ROSE GIFFORD 10

A. J. SHARPE 16

SAMI AKERELE 20

SAMANTHA STOREY 27

BRIANA LYNN SŸ 33

JAMES PAXTON PRIESTLEY 39

DAISY ATKINS 44

KATE STEPANOVA 51

EZRA STEVENS 52

TOBY COTTON 54

ALISON EHRINGER 58

CHARLOTTE BULLING 59

A. J. SHARPE 60

ZAHRA JAMAL 61

AMELIE COMMINS 63

DAISY ATKINS 64

CHERRY LYNNE 65

THE TEAM BEHIND *CROSSROADS* 67

Crossroads

Editor: Iestyn Tudor

Broken Sleep Books

FOREWORD

Personally and collectively, we are at a crossroads. The paths and possibilities ahead are all obscured by darkness. Uncertainty. Suffering. Life in 2025 weighs upon us all. Our living standards are crumbling. Fascism is on the rise. We're witnessing the most-documented genocide in human history. Generative AI continues its onslaught. There's human-led environmental disaster. There's the rollback in women's rights and suppression of LGBTQ+ voices across the globe. There's the worsening wealth inequality worldwide.

It doesn't end. I could go on.

This isn't to mention our personal struggles. The challenges unique to our own lives.

Every source of friction, personal and collective, shapes the way that we write. We are victims of our time and circumstances. This isn't a particularly political collection of writing. But context is important. This is the world we're writing in.

In a world that's becoming increasingly anti-human, literature and art reminds us of who we are.

We agreed upon the title *Crossroads* as a group of postgraduate creative writing students. No subject could be more relevant to our lives. We — the editors and the social media team behind this anthology — are just leaving university. We're growing up in a society that seems to be collapsing. There are absolutely no guarantees for our generation.

But we all have potential. Literature is one of the brightest lights in times of overwhelming darkness, whether it provides escapism or directly confronts our shadow. We hope to showcase the work of new and brilliant voices in this anthology. We thank everyone for their submissions, and encourage those who did not make it into *Crossroads* to continue their creative work. Your voice and your craft are getting there. The world needs stories. It needs poetry. It needs art.

We were pleasantly surprised by the range of prose and poetry sent to us. Each writer has responded to the prompt in their own way. We have fantasy, realism, magical realism, gothic, and comedy stories. Poetry cannot be categorised: it is its own genre, and therefore it has its own section in the anthology. We also accepted art submissions. We have two pieces by Rose Gifford (our art and poetry editor) and one work by Cherry Lynne.

Writing about crossroads may ease our shared anxiety. Profound uncertainty about the future has always been part of human nature. In a literal sense, people have never known where to go throughout their entire lives. Do we stay on the familiar and trodden path? Or, as Robert Frost suggested, do we take the one less travelled by?

Our choice could make all the difference.

The team would like to thank everyone who submitted their work for this collection. We hope you enjoy *Crossroads*.

— Iestyn Tudor, Chief Editor

TRACKS
— Rose Gifford

The sleeper train pulls into Carlisle just as Langston is hanging up a call to his wife. 'Yes, alright, I'll message in the morning. Don't be so crass… you'll wake her up if you keep talking like this…'

He squints against the oncoming glare of the headlights, luminous like cat eyes. The only other passenger emerges from the shadows and into their beam — a young woman with a backpack. She's smiling, or maybe it's just the light. He is resentful of the way the person she's thinking about makes her insular, takes her somewhere else. He steps into the carriage and their eyes meet, briefly, before she looks through him towards something in the distance.

'Room Twenty-Two… Twenty-Two…'

He is the kind of tired that makes everything dance like reflections in dark water, which makes him feel drunk — not that he's touched a drop since she was born. It is on nights like this that he craves it, when the world feels like a zoetrope that won't stop spinning. He pictures himself as one of the silhouetted men, neatly carved, dark against a backdrop of colour.

The train twists beneath him and he lurches towards the compartment door. He scans his key card and stumbles into the tiny room, jettisoning his briefcase. *There* is that strange longing again, the one he can't sate with cigarettes or London meetings or talk of *a bigger house*. A tree flashes outside like a camera bulb and he is reminded strangely of his daughter's hair, not like his or Anna's; those unruly blonde spirals.

His arrival seems to have disturbed his bunkmate. He braces himself. People from the city aren't like people from home. Even when they're walking with you, they're always one step ahead.

'Hiya, mate. Can you see alright?' Before he can reply the man flicks the lamp on, throwing himself into harsh light. He's not what Langston expected — older than him, mid-fifties, perhaps. His accent is coarse like his dad's, like the people he remembers from Inverclyde before they moved.

'Oh, yeah, not to worry…' He extends a hand. 'Langston.'

'Rich.' The train pitches again and he almost falls flat on his face. Rich laughs, and after a moment he does too. He kicks off his dress shoes and loosens his tie. 'Conductor's got it in for us tonight; I haven't slept since we got to Stirling.'

'I haven't slept since I was in London.' He grunts. 'Where are you headed?'

'Home.' Rich settles back down onto the pillows. The conversation appears to be over.

Langston nods to himself. *He shouldn't have said that on the phone. Why did he say that on the phone?*

Rich has his hands clasped over his heart, eyes already closed. Langston dims the lamp and feels his way to his bunk. He stares at the ceiling for a minute, or an hour, watching the lurid reflections of light dancing above him, the roar of the engine following him into his dream. He is sitting in the armchair in the old house, next to the leather sofa, and there is a low sound upstairs, like the wail of a siren. A baby cries. All the while his dad looks just past him, through the window and out to sea.

*

He awakens two hours later to a crude, low, ringing. The engine that lulled him to sleep is gone. It takes him a moment to realise the train has halted. He still feels its phantom movements, like when he was a boy and he swam too far out from the coast — so that the headlands became one improbable shape, and he felt the tide for days after, that endless current, propelling him forward.

'Morning.' Rich's gruff voice floats above the blare over the intercom. After a moment, there's a rap at the door. The conductor shoves it open. 'Sorry folks; just came to say we're having a bit of technical trouble.'

'What kind of trouble?'

The conductor pauses. 'Something on the tracks.'

'The tracks?' Rich sits up sharply. 'Whatever do you mean?'

'I'm afraid that's all I know myself at the moment.'

Langston grimaces. 'I'm… sure you're doing the best you can.'

The conductor nods curtly. 'In the meantime, we've opened up a coffee station in one of the seated cabins. There's a better signal in there too, if you need to contact anyone.' There is a strange relief in this intermission, this state of limbo, that Langston feels overwhelming guilt for.

'Cheers.'

They both make their way, dazed, to the door. Rich's voice is quiet. 'Hope the coffee's still hot.' Neither man says what they are thinking.

*

They sit next to an elderly woman and a teenage boy, no older than eighteen. He is on the phone with his mother. *Yes, I'll message when I'm in Dumbarton. No, they haven't said – probably just a deer or something. Might need you to send me a tenner when I get there.* There is a strange atmosphere in the cabin, akin to a cove before the storm hits.

Langston re-types the text to Anna he has written over ten times. *Sleeper's delayed now. There's something on the line. I'll let you know when we're moving again. I got Lily that book you asked for, the one about the circus elephant, hope it's the right one. Hope I make it back for dinner with Cal and Angela. I'm sorry about snapping on the phone. I was tired. I've missed you. I love you... I've missed you...*

In the corner of the cabin, two women are whispering, one dark haired, one light. *A jumper, I reckon. There's been more and more recently. Al got delayed last month on this line between Motherwell and Watford.*

The rest of the passengers stare resolutely out of the window. It is a rare dawn, golden, clear of mist. A plough makes its slow descent through the fields with wheat in its teeth, shucking the white pearls of raindrops on the glass pane of the window. He reaches for his case notes and is glad to find them missing, stationed beneath the bunk, next to Rich's muddied boots.

'Good morning ladies and gentlemen, apologies again for the delay heading into the West Highlands this morning. The tracks have been cleared and we will be proceeding within the next couple of minutes. Thank you again for your patience.'

Tentative chatter arises again. Some people close their eyes, finally allowing themselves to sleep. There's the girl again, behind the glass panes, her face pink with tears, or sun, he can't tell. She's on the phone, pacing, carding a hand through her light curls. He makes out disjointed words. *No, he didn't meet me here. I'm worried, I've tried texting...* A couple passes her by, their hands conjoined. They don't notice the girl but she looks up, just for a moment.

Langston types *West Highlands Line train disruptions* into Google. The search doesn't send. He is sickeningly relieved. The girl stumbles as the train begins moving again. He should go to her; why is no one going to her?

His phone buzzes in his hand. Anna is calling. He answers it, his eyes still on the girl. 'Langston, hi.' There's a levity in her voice that he hasn't heard in a long time. Trepidation, too. Perhaps she saw something on the news. 'Where are you now?'

'Uh, just leaving Helensburgh.'

'No, I know - you texted me that.' He pictures her biting her lower lip, twisting the phone cord around her long fingers. 'I mean, are you alone?'

'No, I'm in one of the compartments.' He closes his eyes, bracing himself. 'Everything alright?'

She breathes in deeply. 'Could you go back to your room for a sec… oh, you know what? Fuck it.' She never swears. He hears Lily singing in the background. The elderly woman catches his eye and smiles. 'I'm… I just… I had to be sure and I took the test and…' Her words are almost drowned by the engine. 'I'm… we're expecting.'

There's a beat of silence. Half-delirious, he stares up at the cabin ceiling. 'Oh, Anna.'

'I know.' The words are static. They're entering a tunnel. 'I think it's a boy.' 'I'm…How do you know?'

'Just a feeling.' The connection wanes. She says something else that he can't hear.

'Anna… I'm losing you… Anna…' He rushes to encapsulate what he's feeling — the warmth pressing at his ribs, flowering around them. 'I can't wait to be home.' 'Try her again when we get to Crieff.'

Rich stares impassively at the breadth of the Loch outside the window, its hackles raised by the wind. 'Bad signal out here.'

Both men close their eyes. Langston falls into a strange half-dormant state, his body asleep, his mind stubbornly awake. He takes a picture of the sunset at Fort William station. As he waits for it to be sent to Anna, he notices the young girl from the train loitering at the edge of the platform. Her face is motion blurred. She might be smiling at the man opposite her with his arms ajar — her husband, the train signaller, a stranger—

More faces emerge, like film developing in a darkroom. He watches the image buffer and buffer, incrementally, like a child taking their first steps.

WHITHERWARD?
— *A. J. Sharpe*

Four wooden hands stood proudly at the centre of the crossway, circled by a wide ring of small brown mushrooms. The finely carved fingers — complete with dainty nails and thin lines across the joints — pointed in different directions, gesturing across the flower field.

No words were etched upon them.

'Curious,' the Pilgrim muttered to themself, pacing around the signpost. Their eyebrows knitted together as they ran their own fingers across the unmarred wood. 'How entirely unhelpful.'

They turned around, admiring the landscape. The sun hung directly overhead. The Pilgrim wished for a breeze, the light's heat just slightly too stifling. Under a bright cerulean sky, a vast sea of wildflowers stretched in every direction. The heavy scent perfumed the air — a cloying smell that caught in the back of the Pilgrim's throat. The rich blues and buttery yellows of the petals were so violently bright — more saturated than they had ever seen. Four dusty dirt paths led off from the strange signpost, disappearing over the horizon.

Sitting down beside the wooden hands, the Pilgrim frowned. The ground was rougher than expected, lumpy beneath the emerald grass. Sighing, they leant against the wooden pole of the sign and closed their eyes.

Lost? A voice hummed inside their head, cool like spring water.

The Pilgrim trembled. They snapped their eyes open. A dozen people now lay around them. The group lounged in the warm sun, gazing up at the sky with grins on their faces.

Why not stay here?

Something slunk onto the Pilgrim's shoulder, sending a creeping chill down their spine, as though a thin finger was gently tracing each small bone. In the corner of their eye, they could see something dark pulsating by their neck. It shimmered in the sun, as if it were full of bright, white starlight.

'Actually, I should leave.' The Pilgrim began to stand up, shuddering as the creature's body pulsed against their collar bone. 'I'm on my way somewhere.'

Whitherward? What direction will you go?

Twisting around, the Pilgrim stared at the four paths, each stretching out to infinity.

The creature upon their shoulder began to writhe, curling in tighter towards their neck. They could feel its cool flesh thrumming against their skin.

Why not stay here?

The Pilgrim looked around again — the people seemed happy enough, lolling around amongst the daisies.

Stay here.

Stumbling away from the signpost, the Pilgrim shifted clumsily on their feet, uneasy under the weight of the creature. They approached a blonde woman, lying sprawled out on the grass nearby.

They stopped beside her, looking down on her sun-kissed face. 'Excuse me, where were you going?'

'I was going to be a doctor,' she said, her tone soft and dreamy. Her face was still pulled into a taut smile as she spoke. She stared up at the sun with wide eyes, the colour of a summer sky. 'But what if I'm not smart enough?'

It is more comfortable here.

They could feel the creature's plump little body curling tighter into the curve of their neck, pressing harder against them.

The Pilgrim turned to an old man, a silvery beard like fluffy moss billowing out from his wrinkled face. His wizened body was propped up against a rock, his head tilted back to look up at the sky. 'Where were you going, Sir?'

'I was going to be an actor,' the elder said wistfully, gazing up at the glaring sun as though it were a stage light dangling above him. 'But what if they all made fun of me?'

It is kinder here. The creature burrowed in closer, its glittering body throbbing.

Frowning, the Pilgrim strode over to a tall man lounging near the edge of the mushroom ring, his dark skin glowing golden in the sunlight. 'Where were you going?'

'I was going to be a florist,' the man said moonily. His long, fine fingers twirled a blue cornflower between them as he looked up at the sun. 'But what if I failed?'

It is safer here.

The Pilgrim shook their head, looking down at the man with pity.

'What if you hadn't?'

The Pilgrim ignored the angry churning of the creature's body. They looked around at the group, inspecting their faces. The people held their grins tightly, their cheeks pulled upwards as if they were tied with an invisible string, stitched in place. They stared at the people's eyes, glossy with unbroken tears.

'I really should be going,' the Pilgrim said, looking sternly down at the creature draped over them. Its body pulsated rapidly as they pulled it from their shoulder, letting its fat form plop onto the ground among the golden poppies. It wriggled violently, thrashing around in a tantrum. Its tiny mouth snapped at the Pilgrim's feet hungrily.

No! Stay! Its voice boomed inside the Pilgrim's skull. *Whitherward? You are lost!*

'Onward.'

The Pilgrim turned away from the creature, marching down the path to their left. They held their head high and stepped over the ring of mushrooms. A strange popping sound echoed inside their skull, and a feeling of lightness washed over them.

They glanced over their shoulder, back to the signpost. It stood wonky and weathered, choked by the lichen blooming across its decaying wood. The star-lit, black creature was nowhere to be seen, but the acrid smell of sulphur wafted on the wind. The area smelled of rot — a cloying smell again, one that choked the Pilgrim. Scattered around the clearing, among the lifeless flowers and dry brown grass, were patches of sun-bleached bones. Black scrubby weeds wound around the skeletons, tethering them to the spot.

The Pilgrim shook their head and left.

STRONGHOLD
— Sami Akerele

The fortress loomed at the crossroads, its eight marble sides facing distant kingdoms.

Soren tightened the strap on his pauldron. His layered armour shifted with a soft clink as the smooth teal fabric fluttered beneath the polished steel plating. Underfoot, the stone was cool and timeworn, roughened by centuries of guardians pacing the battlements above the portals.

He leant against the wall, eyes fixed on the horizon beyond the fortress's gates, each opening toward a distant land — realms covered in red sand, towering cliffs, frozen forests, lush jungles… Soren grew up hearing tales of these realms from other guardians. But he had never been allowed to step through a gate.

His fellow guardian, Aelin, came up beside him. 'Lost in thought again?' she asked, tilting her head with a wry smile. 'You stare at those kingdoms like they're calling out to you. One day, you'll fall right over the wall trying to follow them with your eyes.'

Soren gave a faint smile. 'Wouldn't be the worst way to go.'

Aelin chuckled. 'For how fed up with your post you seem, at least your humour is intact. Honestly, I'm surprised your father hasn't chained you to the parapet.'

He smirked, though it didn't quite reach his eyes. 'He tried. First, it was endless drills. Then reassignment. I stared at the portals so much, he finally sent me up here. Probably thought I'd run through one someday.'

With a sideways glance, Aelin grinned. 'And now you just brood from a higher vantage. Very dramatic.'

Soren's smile faded. He turned back to the gates. A tense silence fell between them.

'I've been stuck behind these walls my entire life,' he said. 'It feels more like a prison than a home.'

'I don't get you,' Aelin said incredulously. 'You've got the title, the respect, and it was practically handed to you.'

Soren's gaze locked onto the hazy eastern horizon. He let out a breath. 'That's exactly the problem.'

She raised an eyebrow. 'So, you're upset because you didn't have to fight for it? People would kill to wear this armour. Hell, some probably have.'

Soren's expression tightened. 'You all chose to become guardians. My entire life, I was never given a choice. In anything.'

An awkward moment passed between them. Aelin looked away briefly. 'Oh! Meant to say earlier… Your dad wants to see you.' Aelin nodded toward the stairs leading down to the central courtyard. 'He's down there now.'

Soren's breath caught. He looked back toward the horizon, bracing himself. 'What does he want?'

Aelin shrugged. 'Didn't say.'

Soren nodded, his jaw set as he descended the winding stone steps toward the fortress's heart, and toward the man who shaped his life; kept him chained.

As he moved downward, the fortress's hum grew louder. Distant weapon drills, footsteps, muffled conversations, and the deeper thrum of portal magic echoing in chambers far below.

He passed other guardians, nodding to familiar faces. Some

returned the gesture with quiet respect. Others barely acknowledged him. It was no secret that he was next in line for commander, and that he hadn't truly earned it.

At the base of the steps, the corridor curved into the central hall. Commander Varek stood by a round command table, arms crossed, and scanning a large map showing courier routes and garrison placements.

Varek looked up, his voice firm. 'You're late.'

'I wasn't told to run,' Soren replied evenly.

Varek's eyes narrowed beneath heavy brows. 'Discipline isn't just for drills. It's how we measure those who wear this armour.'

'I didn't realise this was a test.'

'It always is.'

A heavy silence settled with suppressed emotion, and all the words left unsaid.

'You didn't call me down here to lecture me about timing,' Soren finally said.

Varek gestured to the map. Dotted lines traced through the eastern border, marked with arrows and notations.

'Our scouts report increased activity beyond the eastern threshold,' Varek said. 'Raiders, mercenaries, we're not sure.'

Soren leant over the map, then looked up. 'And what does that have to do with me?'

'I want you to lead the next watch rotation at the eastern gate. I'll be heading out with a small unit to investigate.'

Soren frowned. 'Isn't Malcom assigned to that rotation?'

'I'm replacing him with you.'

Soren narrowed his eyes. 'Because I'm next in line? Or because you don't trust me anywhere else?'

Varek's face remained still. 'Because if something gets through, I want someone there I can count on.'

Soren stepped back. 'You mean someone you can control.'

'This isn't about trust or control,' Varek snapped. 'It's about protecting the fortress. The gates need someone reliable.'

'Someone obedient.'

Varek sighed. His voice softened just slightly. 'I keep you here to protect you.'

Soren's hands clenched. 'Protect me? I'm trapped behind these walls with a title I never asked for. This isn't protection. It's punishment.'

Before Varek could answer, a low, deep bell tolled through the corridors.

Soren froze. 'The eastern gate.'

Varek straightened. 'They've come sooner than expected.'

They ran.

Guardians surged into position, weapons drawn. From a collapsed tunnel under the outer gate, dozens of intruders flooded the courtyard, armed with warclubs, swords and other bladed weapons.

'They've breached the outer wall,' Varek muttered, drawing his blade. 'Stay with the second line. Hold until I give the signal.'

A scout burst from the corridor, panting. 'Some broke through! Heading for the portal chamber!'

Soren's chest tightened. If they reached the portals, every realm connected to the fortress could be at risk. He hesitated, then turned and sprinted.

'Soren!' Varek's voice thundered behind him. Soren didn't look back.

He raced through winding halls, the clash of steel fading behind him. The passage sloped downward, deeper into the fortress's ancient foundations, toward the portal chamber. Normally sealed and patrolled by two guardians, it now stood eerily open.

The vast circular chamber was lit by faint arcane torches, flickering blue along the curved walls. At its heart rose five ancient portals, obsidian arches veined with glowing blue runes. The veins pulsed faintly. The stone's surface shimmering like water held in place by magic, inert, but ready. Within each stood a pane of green liquid-like energy, shimmering faintly like a wall of pale light, gently swirling as if stirred by wind.

Four intruders stood before them. Their backs were to Soren as he snuck forward and drew his sword. The nearest intruder turned and let out a gasp, alerting the others, just as Soren struck him with a lethal blow.

Another lunged at Soren. His blade lacerated Soren's side, steel cut through armour and flesh. Before Soren could retaliate, a third attacker slashed Soren's right thigh as the other's maul slammed against Soren's chest. Pain erupted through his ribs as he was knocked back.

Soren staggered onto his feet, breath shallow, blood dripping down his leg.

He roared and charged forward, decapitating the maul-wielder. Spinning towards the next, Soren delivered another fatal blow. As the final intruder ran towards the portal, Soren lunged and tackled him to the ground, before driving his sword down through the intruder's torso.

Varek arrived moments later to find his son battered and surrounded by bodies. The portals were untouched. Their eyes met briefly before Soren collapsed, blood loss and exhaustion finally overtaking him.

Soren awoke to warm lantern light and the scent of herbs. Bandages wrapped around his chest and thigh. His entire body ached.

Varek was sitting at the edge of the bed. 'You gave us quite a scare,' he said hoarsely. 'You went against orders.'

Soren turned his head. 'I couldn't let them reach the portals,' he groaned, pain clear in his voice.

After a strained pause, Varek placed a hand on Soren's shoulder. 'Maybe it's time I trust you to protect yourself,' he said, his voice tight. 'You have my blessing to leave, son. Find your path.'

Soren's throat tightened. 'Thank you… Father.'

For the first time in ages, Varek smiled. 'Go. Come back when you're ready.'

Two weeks later, Soren stood before the ancient portals, finally feeling free. More than that — excited and confident, too. Pale golden light bathed the courtyard. His attire was lighter now, better suited for travel, with a satchel over one shoulder.

Aelin approached, her usual smile tempered with something softer. 'So,' she said, 'finally taking that leap you've been dreaming about?'

Soren smiled. 'It's time.'

She bumped his shoulder. 'Don't come back too soon.'

He laughed. 'No promises.'

The guardians began the activation sequence. The veins of the centre portal shimmered, pulsing like a heartbeat. The pale, liquid-like energy at its core twisted and brightened, spiralling into a vortex of emerald light streaked with gold. A low hum filled the air. It climbed steadily in pitch before sinking into a deep vibration they felt in their bones. The stone beneath their feet trembled. Magic pressed against their skin, a sudden shift in pressure, as if the air itself came alive.

Soren took a deep breath, smiled and stepped forward.

STRANGE ENCOUNTERS
— Samantha Storey

Andy opened her eyes at the sounds of doves rustling about in the oak trees above her. The early morning light streamed through the branches and moss, casting a kaleidoscope of bright fragments over her tanned skin.

Her white t-shirt was bloodied where she had been stabbed by a particularly vengeful grifter not too long ago.

She closed her eyes again and curled herself into a tighter ball beneath the towering oak, running a hand over where her wound should've been.

I'm still here, huh?

She picked herself up, rising to her feet and brushing off the dirt her body had collected overnight. Dew drops flecked the ground, coating the park in a thin sheen of grey. Her feet were wet. Andy was starving — and cold for that matter, too. It was her fifth year of homelessness. She never had a home in the New Orleans foster care system, either. It had been three weeks since she'd escaped.

Andy held herself and weaved through the brush to get to the pathway. It was breakfast time. She walked towards the exit of the park, careful not to make eye contact with the other stragglers who called this area their 'home'.

She had to move just last week, trading the shelter down Canal for the open air of the city park. Too many men made eyes at her in there. Most of them stared harmlessly from their bedposts, but some would wink at her or brush their hands over her prone figure in the dark, while they moved about during the night deciding which of yesterday's pretty faces to mar. It was only a matter of days before she was next. That's what she told herself before the stabbing.

Andy started to relax a bit as she followed the smell of baked goods being switched in and out of the ovens over at Hattie's Place. They didn't know it served as her secret pantry.

Andy continued down the street, reaching the alleyway between Hattie's and the computer parts shop. She stopped just before the entrance, catching a faint conversation between two people. One man stood in the alleyway, talking to someone that Andy couldn't see. They were probably getting in a smoke before opening time. But Andy didn't smell tobacco. Instead, there was the smell of something herbaceous yet floral, mingling with the scent of buttery pastry dough. Perfume.

Andy heard one of them raise their voice, suddenly agitated. The smell of herbs became stronger. Whilst the spat continued, Andy went to grab herself some baked good rejects from the trash.

There was the sound of quick-moving heels.

The perfumed stranger appeared. A box of discarded goods fell from her hands, landed at her feet. Her eyes widened before she stepped over and gripped Andy's wrist.

'These are for my daughter!' Andy huffed at the aggravated Hattie's employee.

'Ma'am, I don't care who they're for. You can't be rummaging around like that! This is the second time this week. Get out of here, lady, or I'm calling the cops!' The woman had a strong grip — too strong. Andy froze in place.

Cops. Now I really don't want any part of this.

Andy struggled from the woman's grip.

'Hey, let me go, I don't know y-!'

The woman placed her free hand on Andy's mouth. She smiled

coolly and said, 'Come now, don't be like that.' She turned to the other employee. He was growing increasingly impatient, his hands outstretched, as though still locked in the argument Andy had overheard.

The woman turned back to him. 'Chuck, Hattie said last night just before closing that the linoleum in the dining area needs to be mopped up!' The woman contorted her face into a patronizing frown, her eyebrows curling upwards. 'You wouldn't want your boss to be disappointed with you this morning, would you?'

Andy continued to wriggle herself free. Her eyes darted fast between her captor and the employee who went from irritated to obedient in an instant.

'Goodness, you're right! Let me see to that. Don't worry about the goods…' He pointed at the white box that the woman had dropped during their argument. '…they're all yours,' he beamed. He gave a friendly wave before heading towards the cafe's backdoor.

Andy stopped resisting, utterly confused.

'Wha-'

'Now, don't worry about what you just witnessed.' The woman loosened her grip. Andy stepped away. 'Don't ask questions that you don't wanna know the answers to. Here,' the lady picked up the box of discards. She fished a piece of donut from the box and waggled it in her face. 'Want some?'

Andy wanted nothing to do with this woman. All she wanted was to run in the other direction… but her hunger betrayed her.

'…sure.' Andy hesitated, slowly accepting the donut piece.

The woman didn't just act strange. She looked the part, too. She wore a tattered purple skirt and a grey wool sweater.

She must be baking in that thing, Andy thought.

'Come. Walk with me and share the rest? There's too much in here for one person.' She looked Andy up and down. 'I'm Purcilla, by the way.'

This lady is crazy.

'...um, alright, Purcilla. I'm Andy.'

'Well, it's nice to meet you, Andy. Thanks for letting me use you for a spell like that.'

Andy swallowed a chunk of donut and turned to Purcilla. 'You didn't give me much of a choice.'

'You're right. My bad.' Purcilla stopped to study her face suddenly. 'You look like you might understand the desperation of a lady in need.'

Andy couldn't argue with that. 'I suppose. Hey, how did… how did you make that guy just leave us be back there? It doesn't make any sense.'

'Uhp-uhp-uhp,' Purcilla quickly tutted. 'Remember what I told you?'

'Yeah. No asking questions I don't want the answers to. Tell me anyway.'

Purcilla stopped and gestured at a bench about twenty feet ahead. 'Then let's sit for a minute.'

Andy sat on the bench. Purcilla gathered her skirt neatly behind her as she lowered herself.

'I'm a witch,' Purcilla said. Her face was straight, her tone deadpan.

Andy rolled her eyes and laughed at Purcilla's serious delivery.

'If you're a witch, then I'm a vampire,' Andy scoffed.

'I'm serious, honey. I'm only sharing that with you because you look like you need a home. That's not everything I can see that you need, either. Your sour expression tells me you're hiding something beneath it.'

'What are you saying?' Andy had stopped laughing now.

'Did you think I wouldn't notice? Your shirt's bloody at the hem. But look, there's no wound. You're a witch. And a covenless one, at that.'

Andy contorted her face and opened her mouth as if to say something back. But all that escaped her lips was a quiet gasp. There was something off about her and she knew it.

Andy sighed. 'I can heal myself. I've been able to do that since I was young. I'd get scratches while playing outside. They'd fade away in a flash. I… I just assumed I had some medical condition, or something.'

Andy couldn't believe in the occult, let alone grapple with her own misery. She didn't have the luxury of thinking about anything else except survival. She'd heard old wives' tales about strange things happening out in the bayous, but plenty of strange things happened out there anyway. Like the recent Doogler murders.

The siblings' bodies were just found last week. Andy had read it in the paper one afternoon outside the corner store on Elysium. She still couldn't forget the images of those two little girls adorned in matching bows and ribbons. The thought of them both floating face down in the St. John haunted her at night. She hated herself for not knowing if it was because she felt sorry for them, or for the possibility she might end up just like them too if she continued living like a vagrant.

Andy started to cry.

Purcilla offered her hand.

'Come with me. You can have a home now.'

Between tears, Andy stared at Purcilla's hand before looking back at the park entrance across the street. Surprising herself, she reached for Purcilla's hand without hesitation, hanging on tight.

The two of them stayed in an embrace on the bench for a while until Andy pulled back, wiping her eyes with her palms.

'So, what is your power, like possessing people's minds or something?'

'Something like that,' replied Purcilla with a soft smile.

They broke into laughter.

ROADS THAT WON'T UNDO
— Briana Lynn Sÿ

Millie turned the knob in an effort to get the air blowing, but it was still going in and out. Only hot air blew at her face. She tied her hair into braids, undoing them, then braiding them again. She turned on the radio and sang along. Her mama had always wanted her to follow her dreams. Millie pulled out the flyer from her purse: *Join our band! Country singer wanted! Open Auditions July 8-10, Los Angeles, CA.* Traveling across the country wasn't exactly what Mama had in mind for Millie chasing her dreams, but she was happy nevertheless.

She looked through the hotel's window to see Bradley flirting with the young receptionist lady at the front desk, her hand going up his arm.

Millie could envision herself grabbing the gun in the car and going inside to point it at the woman, screaming *'Who are you, grabbin' my man?'* or *'I'll shoot your goddamn head off right now, lil' bitch.'*

But, of course, Millie wouldn't do that. She'd checked out long ago. At that point, she simply needed him to drive her across the country. She couldn't care less if he slept around as much as his little member's heart desired. Once she got to California, she'd find a way out. The receptionist was still a whore, though, and he was too.

Millie scooted herself into the driver's seat and turned the car off. It was a '99 Toyota Avalon that Bradley got for three thousand dollars, off some guy selling it on the side of the road back in Florida. The guy was originally selling it for thirty-five hundred, but Bradley went off with him and came back with the keys in hand. Millie had long learned not to question when Bradley mysteriously got his way.

She got out of the car and slammed the door, not just because she was irritated, but because slamming it was the only way it would properly shut.

She realised she'd forgotten her cigarettes. She leaned into the car through the window and grabbed her purse for the pack and her lighter.

'God dammit.' She flicked her thumb, but no spark.

Across the street was a gas station, chipped yellow paint on the *Gas 'N Go* sign. *$2.14 for reg.* and *$2.31 for prem.* Millie had a twenty in her purse, a late birthday gift from Bradley who told her to get something nice. Something nice as in: get a tank of gas for the car when they inevitably get stuck on the side of the road, and Bradley will go '*Still got that twenty I gave you?*' and of course, Millie will have it because she predicted it all. Millie was like that to Bradley, a backup who was useful when his terrible actions had consequences. And of course, Bradley didn't like consequences.

A bell rang over Millie's head when she stepped inside the gas station. A fan swivelled on the counter with blue streamers blowing. The man behind the counter nodded at her, but stayed sat in his chair reading a newspaper.

The aisles were stocked to the brim, cluttered, but at least somewhat organised. Sure, it was messy, but things had their general place. Millie glided her fingers over the chip bags as she walked. By her feet, an orange, fluffy cat napped on top of bags. She knelt to stare at it, putting her hand over its nose so it could smell her. It perked its head up, sniffed her fingers, then looked at her hand with indifference.

On the walls were walk-in refrigerators filled with cans and bottles of sodas, waters, teas, and coffees. Millie was a smart girl, smart like everyone else. The smart thing would be to get water, because it was healthy, and it was over ninety degrees outside. It would be smart to get water so she wouldn't collapse due to dehydration. If she did, someone would have to call an ambulance. With twenty bucks in her pocket, they sure as hell couldn't afford neither ambulance ride nor a visit to the hospital just for them to tell her she's dehydrated. And then, once they were alone, Bradley would put his hands on her again.

Millie, fighting the urge to do the right thing, compromised and grabbed a diet.

She made her way up to the front of the shop, stopping to check out a sunglass stand. She tried on a leopard print pair and looked at her reflection in the smudged mirror. When she took them off, only her sullen eyes stared back at her. Behind a glass cabinet were purple pill packets reading: *Get Hard Fast! Lasts for Four Hours.* Who can go at it for four hours? Bradley could get the job done in four minutes, tops. Under the counter were candy bars and gum. Right next to them were keychains in the shape of states, with backgrounds of the Texas and American flag. Some read, *Howdy Ya'll!*

Millie went up to the register. The guy stood.

'Can I get a lighter?' she asked, motioning to the row behind him.

'Which one?'

'Whichever.'

He grabbed a pink one.

On the counter were pepper sprays covered with bedazzled gems. $10.99.

Not too bad.

When Millie walked out, the bell above her jingled. She stuffed the plastic bag in her purse and lit up a cigarette.

She stood by the gas pumps. One had an orange cover on it with a paper reading, *out of order,* stuck on with a single piece of tape. That piece of tape was holding on for dear life. Any gust of wind, and that paper would be long gone.

Down the road, two streets converged to the one in front of Millie.

She was at a crossroads.

She could feel herself coming undone. Roads, for the most part, could never be undone. They always stay the same, leading to the same paths. Millie just didn't know which one to take.

Maybe some dreams weren't meant to be achieved. Had she stayed home in Florida, she wouldn't be in the middle of nowhere, Texas, with her cheating boyfriend who was probably finishing inside that receptionist right then. Had she stayed home in Florida, she'd be at home with Mama and Daddy. Mama would serve dinner of her delicious brisket and cornbread, and Daddy would finally teach her how to shoot a pistol. It was a good thing Millie was a visual learner; she could probably figure it out.

Bradley came out of a hotel room holding his jeans up by the crotch. He looked inside the car.

'I'm over here,' she called, making her way over to him.

'Listen, I'm short on cash for the room. You still got that twenty I gave you?' He made the face that meant he was lying, his smile crooked.

Millie smiled weakly. 'Sorry. I just spent some of it at the gas station.'

'At the-' He huffed and stepped close to her face. 'You spent my money? What did you buy?'

'A lighter, and uh...' She put her hand in her purse, preparing herself, 'And a soda. But it's diet, so you know, uh, no cavities.'

'I don't give a damn about no cavities, Mildred. Now get on, I got us a room.'

Bradley had been drinking. Where he got the alcohol, Millie didn't know. She was curled up against the headboard, knees tucked to her chest.

'Where's the change?' He put the beer can down and went over to her purse, dumping everything out and onto the table. 'That's six dollars. That damn soda and lighter should not have cost that much. What else did you get?'

'I don't know, maybe he miscounted.'

'Bullshit! Tell me, Mildred!'

He took the gun out of his pocket and stomped toward her.

Millie grabbed the bedazzled pepper spray from her back pocket and sprayed him in the eyes.

He cried, slouching to the ground. Getting up to her feet, she grabbed the car keys on the counter and ran out the door. She jumped down the stairs and got into the car, shoving the key hard in the ignition and twisting it a few times before the engine rumbled. She backed into the street and was faced with the crossroads.

The one on the right was the road they came down from, where they came from. Florida.

The one on the left would take her back on the freeway, towards California.

Millie stopped, hesitating. She couldn't deny those dreams that still clung to her. She could still picture herself up on that stage singing her little heart out.

Millie hit the gas.

BARGAIN AT BLACKWARDINE
— *James Paxton Priestley*

I am a writer with a longstanding interest in folk horror and weird fiction. I was thrilled, therefore, when I learned that the Department of English and Creative Writing had opened prose and poetry submissions for inclusion in this MA anthology.

You'll understand why I became so excited upon learning that the theme was 'crossroads'. My mind turned at once to folklore crossroads myths about making deals with the Devil. However, I suffered such a visceral reaction to the idea of writing something that I remained in a troubled state of mind for days. The reason? I had fashioned a subconscious bridge between this first-rate publishing opportunity and an unsettling personal incident from last year.

This tale demands I share a sample of something written by someone else, for although we have never met, there is a bond of knowledge between them and myself. As I share with you what I know of this 'other', you will understand my initial reluctance to submit this piece. My account will be brief, as it would unsettle me to share too much.

I appreciate how melodramatic and cryptic this must sound to you — though, being now in my mid-sixties, I trust you will forgive my insensitivity when I say I'm too long in the tooth to give much thought and weight to what others think of me. I mean no offense. That said, I acknowledge the tale I shall relay to you does, on the surface, sound fanciful. My occasional ruminations on the incident still bring to my mind a thought-provoking observation made by H. P. Lovecraft in his 1931 novella *The Shadow Over Innsmouth*, where he wrote: 'After all, the strangest and maddest of myths are often merely symbols or allegories based upon truth.' I decided that my story could be no more fanciful than something penned by Lovecraft, so proceeded. Take and make of this what you will.

That said, I urge caution, for indeed this tale requires it. I assume no responsibility of the outcome for any who act on the intelligence I offer here but, in wishing ill to none, I have withheld critical facts to safeguard those who *might* act on what I divulge.

Last year, I had driven to Hay-on-Wye to rummage through the myriad second-hand and antiquarian bookshops that spring upon you from around every corner. As must be the case with every bibliophile, I soon experienced a sensory overload, having skipped from one specialty bookshop to another.

After lunch, I headed for the primary target of my visit: The Addyman Annex at 27 Castle Street. I had enquired and been told they had a good second-hand copy of *An Exorcist Explains the Demonic: The Antics of Satan and His Army of Fallen Angels*, the 2016 paperback by Father Gabriele Amorth, Rome's renowned exorcist. There were, of course, other books on demonology, witchcraft and the like which I was on the lookout for. But had I secured Fr. Amorth's book alone, I would have been quite content.

As good fortune would have it, I came away with a weighty haul of research material, including the accounts of Fr. Amorth. A day well spent. I returned to my home in Aberystwyth.

It was not until the next day, while flicking through the pages of Fr. Amorth's book, that I discovered a folded hand-written note about midway through.

I could not establish how long it had nestled between those pages — a day, a month, several years — because name and initials were absent, as were date and place of origin. The paper was in fine enough condition and did not seem of unusual stock. A fountain pen may well have been the instrument from which the black handwriting arose. I read the contents of the note several times, and concluded that it was an elaborate prank. Who penned it? Perhaps I'll never know. Why this book? If inserted in a mindful way, I can only postulate that the note's contents applied to the book's subject, and vice versa. Although I doubted the authenticity of the note, re-reading it unsettled me, physically and mentally — *especially* when uttering aloud the Latin I present below... the second part of which (for there were two lines of Latin invocation) I have omitted for safety reasons.

Although it was closer to midday than midnight, and with Samhain yet some way off, I sensed the wavering company of a formless presence and felt 'pulled', for want of a better word, in a direction east. It is one of the oddest things I've read, and I share now, verbatim, the parts I feel it safe to provide. Please keep any thoughts about the contents of the following note, and my commentary, to yourself, for I do not wish to have you share them with me:

> At Samhain, on 31st of October, when the veil is at its thinnest, travel to the Blackwardine Crossroads, situated west of the small community of Humber in Herefordshire. Coordinates: 52°12'06.2"N 2°41'11.2"W.
>
> Stand at the road's edge, close to the hedge in the south-east corner of the crossroads near the multi-destination street sign. On the other side of the hedge is a standing stone, which sits astride a ley line. Align yourself with the stone. At the hour of midnight, speak aloud (in the precise order shown) these two lines of summoning invocation in Latin:
>
> Daemonem huius loci invoco ut prodeat et desiderium cordis mei mihi concedat.
>
> [*Me: here, the author had written a second line of Latin.*]

This translates to 'I invoke the demon of this place to come forth and grant me the desire of my heart; and…'

[Me: the author of the note then translated the second line of Latin.]

If you have adhered to the contents of this note without deviation, and the crossroads demon deems you worthy, they will appear — as they did to me. Note: its form will never be the same for any two people; it is pointless, therefore, for me to provide such descriptive details, or to prepare you for what will transpire, for human wants and needs are never identical.

Take heed: the demon may grant your wish but *will* expect something in return. Are you prepared to pay the price? The rewards are significant… but the costs may well outweigh the benefits.

[Me: the author of the note ended with certain follow-on instructions and a brief prayer. I flipped the note over, expecting more to be written on the reverse, despite already knowing it was blank. Why do we do that?].

Had I accepted the note as genuine, I would have wondered how the composer gained their knowledge — and what may have become of them upon striking their Blackwardine Crossroads bargain with the demon. Was this note testimony to their survival and continued wellbeing? Or had someone (or something) else inserted the note in Fr. Amorth's book? I took a photo of the note with my iPhone to safeguard against losing or misplacing it, then folded it and tucked it in the rear of the book.

In October last year, my partner and I drove east from Aberystwyth in search of the Humber Woodland of Remembrance in Herefordshire, having discovered they offer green burials. We'd been making preparatory plans for some time for our eventual resting place. I'd used my iPhone to navigate us there (yet I felt certain of the route, as though guided by some unseen hand) and hadn't bothered to establish what else of interest might be in the vicinity of our intended destination. We approached the Woodland of Remembrance from the south, having driven north through Hereford via the A49 and A417, then taken the Bowley Lane north.

After we'd parked at the entrance to the site (which was closed, as expected, for that time of year) and strolled up Bowley Lane to reach the north-west corner of the grounds, I glanced across and saw a standing stone sited in the corner, pointing upwards from the earth like some stone giant's finger.

The pit of my stomach flipped. I took a sharp intake of breath. With pupils no doubt the size of saucers, I spun around to take in a 360-degree scan of my surroundings. We were at the south-east corner of two intersecting roads.

I scrambled for my iPhone and checked my photo library for the image I'd taken of the note I'd discovered in the book. Upon enlarging the image, I checked the coordinates with Google Maps. We were now standing at the Blackwardine Crossroads, almost directly under the multi-destination road sign.

My partner appeared justly bemused by my inexplicable haste to depart and return home.

THE DEVIL LOVES SPORTS DAY (AND GYM SHORTS)
— *Daisy Atkins*

Arthur Williams would have sold his soul for a Subway sandwich. In fact, he would have sold an arm and a leg, too, because missing a soul wasn't enough to get him out of PE. There were a lot of things Arthur desperately wanted, but a Spicy Italian would do for now.

Amber Weston giggled. Yep, she'd definitely written that when she was twelve. Sarcastic and dark-humoured was her *thing* in high school. She had found the notebook shoved down the side of her bed when she was cleaning out her childhood bedroom. It was an old pink rough book, the kind teachers handed out during wet break to keep kids busy. The cover was battered, with DO NOT READ scrawled across the top in lopsided red bubble writing.

Written inside were the many exploits of poor old Arthur Williams, a self-insert who'd ended up in a battle with the devil for his soul.

Now it lay cracked open on her desk. The writing stopped halfway down the page. She had ignored it for a while, busy hoovering and organising and bagging her old clothes to sell, but something was drawing her towards it.

There was a time in Amber's life when the idea of an unfinished story would have been unbearable, when she would have stayed up all night just to fight her way to an ending. But somewhere along the way, through college, university and jobs, she'd stopped needing to know the endings. She'd stopped believing they were hers to write.

Amber couldn't remember the last time she'd started a story, let alone finished one, but somehow she found herself sitting down at her old desk and opening up a new Google Doc. She stared.

The cursor blinked, mocking her: *You can't write anymore.*

It was right. She slammed the laptop shut.

'Uh, rude!' Came a voice behind her.

Amber screamed, jumping up out of the chair.

She grabbed the nearest object to her, which happened to be her old bejewelled pink stapler, wielding it like a weapon.

'Oh great,' said a chubby boy sitting on her bed, rather dryly. 'You're gonna kill me with kiddie office supplies? That's even worse than the devil stealing my soul whilst wearing *Crocs*.'

He was perched casually, legs swinging like he owned the place. In his lap lay a small, wooden box with strange symbols carved into it. He waved and said, 'Hello, Amber L. Weston!'

'Who the hell are you? How do you know my name?'

'Uh, maybe because it's written across the front of my *life!*' The boy pointed at the notebook. 'I also know you wrote 'Mrs Amber Carter' next to lots of little hearts, but I'm guessing *that* never happened.'

Amber dropped the stapler, marched over, grabbed his arm and practically threw him out of the room.

She exhaled sharply and spun back around.

He was back on the bed.

'Rude,' the boy said, unfazed. 'You just *yeeted* a twelve-year-old out the door.'

'Get out of my room!' Amber growled, going to grab him again. 'How did you do that?'

'Lady, don't ask. I don't know.' The boy made a face. 'Seriously? You don't recognise me?' He gestured down to himself, pointing at the school emblem on his bright yellow t-shirt.

She shook her head desperately. 'Should I?'

The boy looked deeply offended, then rolled his eyes dramatically. 'Okay, Ms. Creator. I see how it is. You create me, make me a fat loser, make me suffer through PE all summer, force me to eat gruelling school dinners, sell my soul to the literal *Prince of Darkness*, and then forget me? Real nice.'

Amber blinked. And then blinked again. 'Wait. What? *Arthur*?'

'Ding ding ding! Correct! Give the woman a degree! Oh, wait, she already has one! In *Creative Writing,* nonetheless. And she still couldn't be bothered to *finish my story*!' He raised his arms and drew a rectangle in the air. '*The Devil Loves Sports Day – and Gym Shorts.* What a great title to rot in literary purgatory forever. I should sue for emotional neglect.'

Amber stared as, slowly and impossibly, the boy became familiar. The blue eyes. The sulky glare. The sarcasm. 'But— you're not real!'

'Oh, jeez.' Arthur rolled his eyes again, tutting. 'Let's just move past that already. Believe me, I've had a decade to grapple with the metaphysical implications of my existence. I'm over it.'

Amber opened her mouth, then closed it again. She wasn't sure if she wanted to laugh or cry.

'Okay. But why are you here?' She asked, rubbing at her eyes. 'Oh, God. I've actually gone mad, haven't I?'

'I knew you'd be like this,' Arthur muttered. 'Can we skip this bit? Look, *writer-girl*, all I want to know is why you started writing me and then just… well, left me there. Mid-sentence. Mid-*deal with the Devil.* Do you know how long it's been Thursday in my world? Ten years! Ten years stuck in these bloody gym shorts! How would you like to be twelve forever?'

'I'm sorry,' was all she could think to say.

'You're sorry? That's it? *You* wrote me! You made me this fat!' He jabbed at his gut. 'You gave me a best friend who eats glue, a dad who works in an abattoir and an ex-military gym teacher who likes to make us do 'motivational screaming' before dodgeball!' He paused, his chest rattling and wheezing. 'You made me hate myself so much I tried to sell my soul to the devil, FOR A SUBWAY SANDWICH and then you made the devil—' He pulled an inhaler out from his pocket and took three quick puffs. '—an *asshole!* Seriously, my characterisation was a mess. I thought I was supposed to sell my soul to *win* Sports Day? That's what the title implies! I bet you forgot all about that abandoned chapter at the back of the notebook where you made me realise I was a fictional character. *That's* why I'm even here! Because *you* wrote it!'

Amber sank back onto her chair, stunned. 'I didn't know anything I wrote could…'

'Come to life? Yeah, writers always think that. Where else would all the energy go?'

'I'm not a writer,' she said. 'I might have a degree, but you're right. I never bothered to finish your story because it sucked. *I* sucked.'

'Well, yeah, the ending you had planned did suck,' Arthur shot back. 'But you don't suck at writing. You were funny before you got all serious with your "themes."' He made quotation marks in the air. 'Honestly, you were much cooler when you didn't care so much. When you made the Devil wear Crocs.'

'You complained about that a minute ago!'

He shushed her. 'Lady, I've been facing that fashion disaster every day for the last ten years; I *earned* my complaints.' Arthur thrust the wooden box into Amber's hands. 'Here, take it.'

She turned it slowly over in her hands. 'What's in it?'

He scratched his head. 'Well, I've had an infinite amount of Thursdays, and a boy can only take so much, so I wrote the ending for you. You gave me the vocabulary, after all.' He grinned. 'Look. I get it. I do. You grew up, got busy, got a degree, got a boyfriend, lost a boyfriend. You got sad. You stopped caring about stories with glue-eating sidekicks and weirdo demons obsessed with gym shorts. But *I* didn't. I never got to grow up. You left me behind. So sue me for being salty about it.'

'So, you're just here to guilt trip me into writing again?'

He crossed his arms, sulking a little. 'So what? I'm a half-finished character from a half-finished story. You owe me an ending. So, finish it, or I swear, I will haunt you every Thursday for the rest of your miserable, washed-up, soul-destroying minimum wage Tesco shift-working life.'

'Ouch,' she laughed. 'You know me well.'

'I *am* you, dumbass.' He pushed himself up off the bed. 'Well, see ya.'

'Wait, you're going now? You've only just-'

'Oh, Amber the Abandoner, give me a break. I know what's about to come for me. I wrote it. Let me get to these crossroads early, alright?'

As Amber opened up the box, Arthur disappeared, simply fading into nothing. Inside was her notebook, the same one that lay open on her desk. Except this one was full. As she flicked through it, she realised it was in *her* handwriting. The box was gone, and there was only one notebook, the one in her hands.

Had she gone insane?

She turned to the last page of the notebook. At the bottom of the page was something written in thick red ink, *not* in her handwriting.

Next time, just make a deal. It's faster that way.

Laughing, she turned her laptop back on and started Arthur's story again.

PIPEDREAM
— Kate Stepanova

You come home late at night,

set your keys down in exhaustion,

shrug off your coat and lean against the wall

under the razor-sharp fluorescent glare.

There is an abscess of an absence

that's eating through your life.

The aimlessness of fighting

to just be left behind.

/

Dim lamplight, smoke, diffusing

through the air like ink,

tinting emptiness a murky grey,

making something out of nothing.

Outside the window, fleeting,

a whisper brushes by:

'You live right at the crossing

of someone else's life.'

THIS WAY
— Ezra Stevens

I come from

      two directions

and neither lets me pass

      without a question.

One asks who I was,

the other

      asks who I am

and neither listens long enough

        to hear the answer.

  There is no map

    for a body

  becoming.

                No arrow for

  'what if,'

        no compass for

'neither.'

But still, I walked—

                              and I arrived.

I am not what was expected

      from every ask,

every direction

           I was pointed.

I am what chose itself

    again and

        again.

SENSES OF PASSAGES
 — *Toby Cotton*

Not so distinct as pied:

not my concrete poems,

not her cowprint jacket

perhaps hopefully lichens,

not dalmatians, more blurred:

porcupine quills left together,

a fizzing moonlit tide

/her faux fur throw,

a box of those chocolates

shaped as swirling seashells

this half-choice,

these potentials

dancing second hands

overlapping minute hands

(my first hands

having sketched out this score)

/those runaway piano keys
dominoing playing infini,
timelapses of games of chess

/timelapses of magpies
accolading their nest

/timelapses of the milky way
from a dark sky reserve

/timelapses of snowmen
being dressed for work

/timelapses of Mont Blanc
undressing down the years

/timelapses of a town high street
on Christmas shopping night

FROM VITALI'S *CHACONNE*
— *Toby Cotton*

The wine-dark rose,

sober, bows low

in such postfusion

of embroidery

how could I forget the rain

the tone poem unfini

my vibrato faltering

harmony of organs

and violin diminuendo

below Gemini, Galilean

quicksands swallow light

only their fledged hearts

but the saxifrage, red veined

white flower of the rock

on the wrong side of

the wind, oh so still

a frequency at which
the vase might fracture

cat scarper, books
unshelve themselves

for this postmodernist
misunderstanding

the string of hearts
at the end of spring
reaches blindly

in the tangible air
for what

It matters not the trill of life,
but this is the piece I would like
played at my finale please by you

KALEIDOSCOPE
— *Alison Ehringer*

At the edges,

pink blends into blue,

rosebud kisses

against cold cheeks;

the faint whisper

of purple

bruises night-time clouds.

Blooming veins

bleed together —

a symphony

played by ear

vehement

in its dissonance.

A shout of maroon

rings through the air,

thick against your tongue:

hard to taste,

harder to swallow,

as you wait

for the absolution

of a clear

bright

sky.

HOLD MY HAND AT THE CROSSROADS
— *Charlotte Bulling*

Hold my hand,

softly. Gently.

Please be delicate

as I stop at this

crossroads. I need

a moment. Just a

wee moment to

make a decision.

To change my identity

in its entirety. Or let

it just be, remaining

just as it is in it's

panicked entirety.

I need you to

hold my hand

at this crossroads.

Just hold my hand

as I make this

decision.

THE DULE TREE
— A. J. Sharpe

Oh — I have seen many an awful act. For years, I sat here, at this forlorn crossroads, forced to dangle people, the bodies slack. Abandoned, the cadaver rots — erodes.

So many lost souls danced their final dance, turning in the soft wind, stung from my bough. The dead forever in an empty trance — their decaying carcass a solemn vow.

Ironic, that they execute them here — a place where paths divulge, choices unfold. Now a place of endings, a place of fear.

No more decisions!

Just left here to mould.

They make this a place of one's last breath, expose the truth of life's fragility. Because what even is death, if not the end of possibility?

WORDS
— *Zahra Jamal*

From one library to another,

From a gathering of kind folk,

folk of the heartspaces between lines of ink,

to the white lights over white tables where

a lone student presses a white keyboard.

Once the change would have disrupted, even distressed.

Now it is a wind around my shoulders, pushing my direction,

pressing the paints into the forms others see.

But only a wind. Beneath is a slow moving sea,

shifting my vision, inking a note

on the back of the canvas just for me.

Words, words, words.

Such strange things,

so careless and small and unable to express.

Even now blindly circling around details

that exist just for the feeling of the moment.

And yet so boundless.

So capable of forming, shaping, breaking

and reconstructing an existence.

Even now carefully revealing the hidden

passageways that lead endlessly into

the spaces beyond words.

Words, words, words.

They lie here,

in the books,

in the structure of the walls

built by conversing workmen,

in the chair I sit upon, used to support

a back as it bends over painstakingly

chosen lines of text,

in the white shapes on my screen,

appearing, disappearing, mocking me.

They lie here

and will lie here evermore

long after us chattering, wordless creatures

have left this shore.

Words, words, words.

I shall lay them to rest

and then disturb them once more.

Every time I move, I breathe, I be,

so shall they be.

ABOUT THE KING'S BEAUTIFUL DAUGHTER
— *Amelie Commins*

In stygian nights, she slips away,

her sunwade gown and crimson beads

scraped off her flesh like rotted clay.

She smears her lovely face with weeds,

dirt staining her sallow cheeks. Coarse

furs and bramble thorns she now

dons, fleeing from her father's force.

Love's baby blossoms are wilted now

and curse this Girl with such sickly

shame that marks her skin and forever

burns. Pilgrim peasant, how quickly

you are barred from gold or pleasure.

Where roads diverge in darkest tide,

you stray alone without a guide.

DEALS THAT CANNOT BE UNDONE
— *Daisy Atkins*

road split into four, the poor man's

doorway into the rich man's land

he only needs a helping hand

he crawls his way towards me

forwards through the mud

his eyes and mouth drip with blood

but i have already planted my

haunted feet in cold hard boots

new forms born in clean black suits

unripened fruit sour sticky residue

hues of green and blue and butterfly traps

old men writhe in burning burlap sacks

in the blackened grass he crawls

and falls and slithers to and fro

crimson slashes bloom and grow

so i throw away unripened fruit

loot and shoot and kill with boots

those forms die in dirty black suits

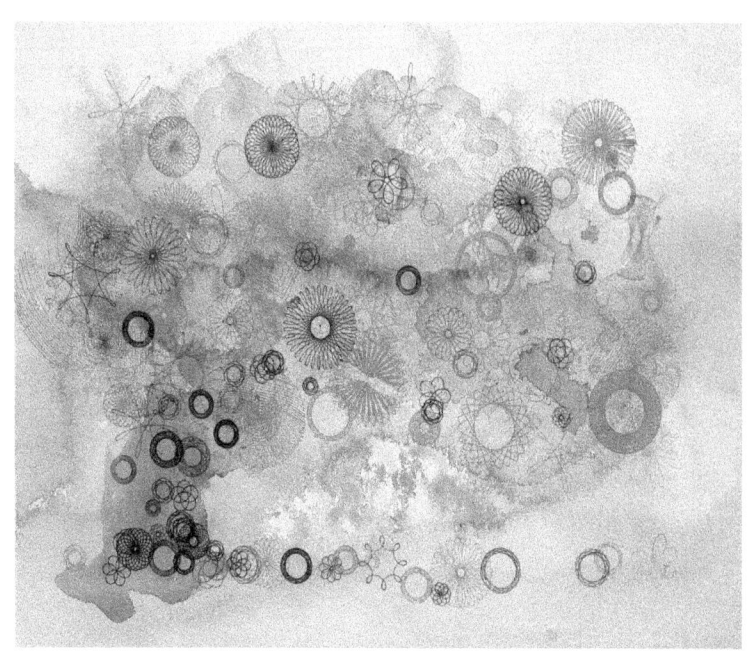

TREE OF LIFE
— *Cherry Lynne*

THE TEAM BEHIND *CROSSROADS*

CHIEF EDITOR — Iestyn Tudor

ASSISTANT CHIEF EDITOR — Aqilah Bte Mohd Badrulhisham

PROSE EDITORS

Briana Lynn Sÿ

Myles Campbell

POETRY EDITORS

Rose Gifford

Iestyn Tudor

SOCIAL MEDIA / OUTREACH

Aqilah Bte Mohd Badrulhisham

Arrabella Kennedy Hughes

Daisy Atkins

LAY OUT YOUR UNREST

www.ingramcontent.com/pod-product-compliance
Lightning Source LLC
Chambersburg PA
CBHW030813090426
42737CB00010B/1256